DANGERous Theologies

Debunking and Fact Checking The Myths, Lies,
and Misconceptions of Traditional Teachings

Dr. A. C. Tulloss, M.Div, D. Min.

www.TrueVinePublishing.org

Dangerous Theologies
by: Dr. A. C. Tulloss

Published by
True Vine Publishing Co. LLC
810 Dominican Dr. Ste. 103
Nashville, TN 37228
www.TrueVinePublishing.org

ISBN: 978-1-962783-83-5 Paperback
ISBN: 978-1-962783-40-8 eBook

ESV: English Standard Version
Scripture quotations marked "ESV" are from the ESV® Bible (The Holy Bible, English Standard Version®), copyright © 2001 by Crossway, a publishing ministry of Good News Publishers. Used by permission. All rights reserved. You may not copy or download more than 500 consecutive verses of the ESV Bible or more than one half of any book of the ESV Bible.

KJV: King James Version
Scripture quotations marked KJV are taken from the Holy Bible King James Version

NIV: New International Version
Scripture quotations taken from The Holy Bible, New International Version® NIV®
Copyright © 1973, 1978, 1984, 2011 by Biblica, Inc. Used with permission. All rights reserved worldwide.

[Scripture quotations are from] New Revised Standard Version Bible, copyright © 1989 National Council of the Churches of Christ in the United States of America. Used by permission. All rights reserved worldwide.

DEDICATION

This book is dedicated, first, to my ancestors on whose shoulders I stand and whose prayers continue to keep me. Then, to my parents Dr. Alvas C. Tulloss, Jr. and Mrs. Gwendolyn B. Tulloss who are among the ancestors, but whose legacy keeps me going. Finally, to all the theology students who refuse to stop learning.

ACKNOWLEDGEMENTS

Thanks goes to Ms. Angie Amonett, MA, my counselor and soundboard of rationality. Thank you for keeping me grounded. Also, thank you to my dear brother in the ministry Dr. Herbert Jenkins and my Friday Fellowship sisters of The Church of Jesus Christ of Ladder Day Saints, thank you all for keeping me centered and for your support through this process.

Table of Content

Prologue

To be abundantly clear, this is not a "Here's what's wrong with the church" book. In fact, I myself have been guilty of perpetuating some bad theologies. Nevertheless, the fact of the matter is that there really is no perfect way to do church. There is only the way prescribed by God to adequately meet the needs of each individual in a given congregation. So, albeit debatable, one could arguably say that there is no wrong way to do church, if in fact the church is God centered and Jesus believing. It is not my intention to get into the varying nuances that modern churches have adopted and adapted, but rather, it is my intention to point out one very important fact: While there may not be a wrong way to do church, there is a wrong way to educate God's people.

In the following pages, I will point out some of these erroneous pedagogies, false teachings, and straight-up lies and show how they have and–if not corrected–will continue to hurt believers, confused Christians, and burned-out church folk. Now, there are many guarantees in life but this one I can make to you, reader, that at least once you will be upset while reading this book. This book may even make you mad a time or two, but keep reading. There is a lot of truth in this book, truth that I hope will indeed set you free.

Lastly, this book is not meant to be an exhaustive list of bad teachings, but rather the beginning of greater insight that can be used to more accurately disciple today's Christians. As leaders in the church, it is important to watch not only what we say to God's people, but one must also watch what we do and the traditions and mandates we set up on God's behalf. These traditions may seem harmless or even like a good idea at the time of institution but they can lead to dangerous theology while trying to appease God in order to have our own agendas met. I'm talking about traditions that sound good but have no sound biblical or theological grounding.

The goal here is to clear up the half-truths of traditional teachings and to dispel the lies that ultimately lead to DANGEROUS THEOLOGIES.

CHAPTER 1

Sugar-Daddy/Santa Claus

For decades, people have been fed cliché and appealing phrases that are misleading and dangerous. These sayings have oftentimes been delivered by well-meaning people, and unsuspecting congregants have pinned their faith in God on these sayings with negative results. Congregants have been led to think that they are standing on a firm foundation, but in reality, they are standing on nothing more than hardened sand. As a result, when the storms and torrents of life hit, their foundation and very relationship with God crumbles, leaving them with nothing more than hurt feelings, disappointment of faith, and a distrust or even hatred of God. Dangerous theologies have led people away from the church, away from God, and away from all things "Christian."

The sad truth is that many church goers have not only fallen victim to cliché sayings and thus develop bad theologies, but some have themselves become perpetrators of the "church-hurt" and the dangerous theologies that they themselves have fallen prey to by repeating cliché sayings and teaching bad theologies to new and spiritually young Christians. I am guilty of this perpetuation too, but now that I know better, I *do* and *teach* better.

Some modern-day teachings are full of lies and misconceptions that are rooted in a time when ignorance could not be avoided and the teachers of the church did the best they could. It was a time when many could not read, could barely read, or were not allowed to read. As congregations and leaders of the church become more learned, we are discovering that a lot of traditional Christian church teachings and sayings are false or misleading. More discussion of these falsities and misconceptions will ensue within the following pages, but before we go any further, let us talk about the word Theology. The Merriam-webster Dictionary website defines theology as[1]:

1. The study of religious faith, practice, and experience
    Especially: the study of God and of God's relation to the world

2. a. A theological theory or system
    b. A distinctive body of theological opinion

3. a usually 4-year course of specialized religious training in a Roman Catholic major seminary

The content of this book will focus mainly on the first two definitions.

---

[1] Theology | Definition of Theology by Merriam-Webster

THE FASTER, THE BETTER

In this fast-paced world where it seems that impatience is the virtue and chaos a steady companion, it has become popular to preach and teach (albeit unintentionally) that there is some kind of secret incantation, dance, tongue, prayer, or shout that can open heaven and manipulate God into immediately doing exactly what we want God to do. Some bad teachings we see surround notions that to receive our desired blessings or outcomes, all we have to do is "name it and claim it," "reach up and get it," pay X amount of money, pray some special prayer, speak some special tongue, or dance some special dance. While sounding good, misleading statements like those can lead to dangerous theologies of God being some kind of wish granting genie that can be easily manipulated or conned into doing OUR bidding in OUR desired time and way.

In our rushing about and distraction-filled lives, we often demand instant service and immediate results. By doing this, we have forgotten that God is sovereign and that God's timing is perfect. God's holy sovereignty means that God does what God wants when, where, how, and to whom God wants. Psalms 115:3 makes this point abundantly clear. It says, "Our God is in the heavens; he does whatever he pleases." Furthermore, scriptures like Exodus 33:19 and Proverbs 19:21 give us clear examples of God's sovereignty. Exodus 33:19 says in part, "...and I will be gracious to whom I will be gracious, and will show mercy on whom I will show mercy." Proverbs 19:21 says, "The human mind may devise many plans, but it is the purpose of the LORD that will be established."

Sometimes in our churchgoing experiences, we hear certain phrases that sound good but (as my friends would say) are "neither scripture nor Bible." Phrases like "You need to sow a seed into this word," or "Cleanliness is next to godliness," or "Your prayers are too small, that's why God isn't answering them. You need to pray big prayers," or "When the praises go up, the blessings come down." One of the worst is "God doesn't hear or answer the prayers of sinners." My problem with statements such as these is that not enough teaching is accompanying them to explain exactly what is meant when they are said. I particularly have an issue with anyone who holds the word of God hostage until they are paid a certain amount of money. If Jesus–the Word himself–never charged for preaching, teaching, or miracle-working, why should we? Now, don't get me wrong. I know that any preacher or speaker needs to be paid for their works, however certain cliché statements like those are rendering people confused by non-scriptural traditions and guilt tripping them out of their hard-earned money. People of God are being plagued by bad and dangerous theologies.

WHEN GOD SAYS "NO"

Now that we know that there is no particular or secret chant, prayer, dance, shout, tongue, or method to conning God into doing what we want, how and when we want it, let's look at why it sometimes does not matter what we do or say, the answer to our prayer is "No." In order to have a healthy, deep, and growing relationship with our Creator, we must first understand God's immense and eternal love for us, and then we must accept God's sovereignty over us and over all of God's creation. This sovereignty means that while God does answer EVERY prayer, sometimes God will give us an answer of "No."

One of the hardest lessons for me to learn as a child was that by saying "No" to me, my parents were showing me that they truly loved me. As a child, that made no sense to me. I thought love meant giving me whatever I wanted whenever I wanted it. I also thought that I could treat my parents the way I would treat my friends. I quickly learned that was not the case. If you had parents like mine, then I'm sure you heard them say something like, "I'm your mother [father], not your friend." While they loved me, and at times were very friendly to me, my parents were wise enough to make sure that I knew the distinct difference between those who truly loved me and those who didn't, as well as the distinct difference between my parents (and other authority figures) and my friends/playmates.

Much like our human parents, God deals with His spiritual children in the same way. God is not our playmate, nor is God in any way our equal. God does not desire to give His children more than they can handle or something that ultimately will hurt them because they were not ready for it. So, whenever God says no, we can always be sure that it is out of love and with our absolute best in mind. The idea of "If you want it, you can have it" and "Reach up and grab it" is simply preposterous. It is a lie and a dangerous theology. Here's the reason why: for a holy parent or even a human being to give a child everything they want just because they asked for is not only dangerous to the wellbeing of that child, it can also cause danger to others around the child as they age into an adult.

The truth is, if God gave us everything we wanted when we wanted it and how we wanted it, we would have no use for Grace, have no patience, and have no real relationship of love with our Holy parent. Now, I too have been on the receiving end of something that I was not yet ready for, and I have found that in those cases God was showing me why He had said "No" to begin with.

There are lessons in life that we only have to learn once because of the pain associated with them. These lessons are brought on by the situations and the circumstances that we have gotten ourselves into. It's not God's fault when we don't listen, nor is it God's fault when we don't accept "No" as a loving rejection or a loving statement of wait. It is our fault. Furthermore, we must remember that God can never be forced, manipulated, or guilted into giving us what we want simply because we want it.

I am reminded of a particular example: I thought I was ready for a certain type of relationship. I wanted to find out what I was missing out on and if the hype about being in love was true. God had (in an unusually specific way) told me not to speak to a particular person and to cease all contact with him. I, instead, felt that I was grown, knew what I was doing, and could handle whatever came from being in a relationship with said person. In the end, I was betrayed, embarrassed, and physically assaulted. I realized then that when God says "No," He means it. And that "No" is not a form of torture or a tyrannical prerogative. Our Holy parent is always loving; just read his love letter called the Bible and you can see that when God says "No," it is out of love and only love. Nevertheless, if we choose to chance it and go our own way, if we choose to pursue that which God has told us is not for us, we will always end up hurt, disappointed, angry, and damaged in some way.

Thankfully though, our Holy parent never rubs our mistakes in our face. Our holy father never says, "I told you so!" or "You should've listened to me in the first place!" (we have our own subconsciousness to do that for us). No, instead we have a loving God who is always ready, willing, and able to pick us up from the lowest of the low, dust us off, and set us back on the right path. Now that's love!

WHEN GOD SAYS "NO"
(Secret Conversations)

We have already discussed some reasons why God says "No" to our requests. Hopefully, you have come to better understand and find peace with the moments in your life where God has answered your request with a "No." At this time, I want to talk to you about a specific kind of "No" that many of us have experienced. One of the most painful "No's" we can ever receive is a "No" to the request of healing a loved one or extending their life on this earth.

First, let me point out a misconception: When God decides to take a loved one away from this earth, it is not necessarily because God has said "No" to your request to heal them. It's not because you did something wrong or prayed the wrong way or not at all, and it is not necessarily because of a lack of faith on your (or someone else's) part. We must understand that when God decides to take a loved one away from this earth, it is because that is what is best for THEM and death is the ultimate healing.

Now, you may say, "How can leaving me be what is best?" This is where the title "Secret Conversations" comes into discussion. Even in the midst of our grief, we must take the time to think about the secret conversations that our loved ones may have been having with God on their own behalf. There is a level of suffering in this life that many can attest to–immeasurable, incurable, torturous, inconsolable pain. This pain is the kind of pain that is often seen by healthcare workers as a person is nearing the end of their life. In my experience, it is during this time, and even in times when patients are comatose, that secret conversations may be occurring between

God and the patient. These are conversations that the outside world is not privy to at the time of utterance. During these conversations, requests are made to God, and we may never know the specifics of those requests, but we can be sure that they have been heard and decided on by God. How do we know this to be true? How do we know that what I have just said about secret conversations is credible? I'm glad you asked. There is a phenomenon among terminal patients that occurs and allows people to get better for a moment, a day, or a few hours–just long enough to say their goodbyes and make their final wishes known. It is in these moments that people have attested to loved ones mentioning (at least in part) these secret conversations. Here are some indicative words and behaviors that give us clues that a secret conversation has occurred:

I'm at peace now....

I'm ready to go....

I'm tired (not the normal tired, but rather, a weariness of life)....

Let me go....

You are going to be ok....

God will take care of you....

It's my time....

God has told me....

God assures me....

God said (Jesus said)....

Everything will be ok....

(Waiting for a specific person or goal before dying)

(The signing of a DNR (Do Not Resuscitate))

(Deceased loved-ones visiting or being seen)

This is by no means an exhaustive list, but merely a list of examples that I have experienced either first hand or second hand during the transitioning[2] of a loved-one or the loved-one of someone I know.

Secondly, it is important for those of us who remain in this life to know and realize that if God has answered our request for a loved-one to be healed, we have to accept God's sovereignty and, we must know that healing takes place in many forms. Eternal healing only occurs after we have left this life and this earth. Temporary healing happens here on earth and is temporary because ultimately everything on and associated with this earth will one day come to an

---

[2] The term *transitioning* here refers to the process of dying. Or, the process of transitioning from life to death.

end. Partial healing can be understood as when part of the symptoms or disease is cured or is in a dormant state. Healings can occur miraculously, spontaneously, completely, partially, or gradually, but ultimate, perfect, and eternal healing only comes after death. All these things being considered, it is quite possible for God's "No" to you to be the result of God's "Yes" to your loved-one. In which case (and I'm speaking even to myself), it is selfish of us to want God to overrule our loved-one's secret requests so that they can stay here on this earth and in this life of suffering just to make us happy.

Here is what we must remember whenever God answers our prayers with a "No." First, we must remember that God is sovereign but not petty. Second, God answers **every** prayer! Third, God's love for us is so deep, so wide, so intense, and so eternal that whatever God does is out of love for us (or in the case of a dying loved-one, out of love for them) and is what is best for us (them). Accepting these truths is vital to having a deep, lasting, and loving relationship with God, and ultimately having peace with God's "No."

CHAPTER 2

God Complex/Savior Complex

In psychology, the word *complex* is defined as:

A constellation of experiences and feelings around a single concept which mediate between one's conscious and unconscious world according to Carl Jung. Complexes shape the manifestation of unconscious thoughts when they press against the ego, such as those in dreams and psychosomatic symptoms...[3]

In layman's terms, a complex is a group of strong thoughts or experiences rooted in one's subconscious but that have influence on one's conscious existence. In other words, if you think or feel something strongly enough, it will influence your behavior and experiences in real-life. So, for a person to have a God Complex or a Savior complex means that they have a literal **NEED** to help or save a person or persons, whether it be detrimental in some way or not. Those who have a God Complex may feel the need to help God.

---

[3] Dictonary of Pasoral Care 6/10/21 *Complex*.

They may feel that they and they alone are needed by God to accomplish a specific task that will result in a person or persons being helped or saved from some perceived threat.

Those who have what is called a Savior Complex typically feel that they are needed and able to save someone or something from danger. People with a Savior Complex often feel the need to help (with or without help being solicited) with no regard for their own wellbeing or the desires of those they "help." They sometimes will literally cause themselves harm or allow themselves to be harmed in order to help by sacrificing their own wellbeing.

> The underlying belief of these individuals is, "It is the noble thing to do." They believe they are somehow better than others because they help people all the time without getting anything back. While motives may or may not be pure, their actions are not helpful to all involved. They are drawn to those who need "saving" for a variety of reasons. However, their efforts to help others may be of an extreme nature that both deplete them and possibly enable the other individual.[4]

That being said, **God doesn't need your help**. Shocking, right? The truth is that the same God who created the universe and everything in it can handle your issues, struggles, mistakes, trials, troubles, situations, problems and more without your help and without your advice. While it is true that God does sometimes use

---

[4] https://www.psychologytoday.com/us/blog/the-high-functioning-alcoholic/201702/the-savior-complex, accessed 08/26/21.

human hands to bring about His divine will, the truth is that even in those cases, God is choosing or has chosen to use human willingness, but not out of need or desperation. So, the truth is that He doesn't **need** our help to help those in need, but God will use humans out of His own prerogative. It is also true that God helps whomever God wants to help, however God wants to help them. That's why God is called sovereign.

And since we are talking about God's help, let's talk about the misconception that "God helps those who help themselves." This is a misconception because the truth is that God helps those whom God desires to help, irrespective of whether or not they can help themselves. God provides for both the just and the unjust, the helpful and the helpless, and teaching that "God only helps those who help themselves" gives birth to a dangerous theology that in turn causes burnout, busybodies, and dissatisfied Christians. Those who live by this misleading teaching often end up disappointed because God does not always help them in the manner they feel they deserve based on how they have "helped themselves." In fact, they wind up committing the sin of Abram and Sarai. These ancestors of the Jews, Christians, and Muslims decided that, albeit, God had made them a promise of a son, they felt that God needed help, so they took matters into their own hands and Sarai gave Abram her handmade Hagar to have a son on Sarai's behalf. In the end, that son was cast away from the son of promise, and their descendants have been at odds ever since.

Furthermore, the theology birthed by the acceptance of the teaching that "God helps those who help themselves" is not only dangerous, but it is a bad theology and a disappointing view of God.

The truth is that God helps those whom God chooses to help and is a champion of those who **cannot** help themselves. In our worst or even lowest moments of life, God has been faithful to step in on our behalf; therefore, we call God names like "Way Maker," "Provider," and "Miracle Worker." This being the case, instead of falling victim to the symptoms of this dangerous theology, it behooves us to trust God to be exactly who God has already been proven to be: our "Helper," "Sustainer," and so much more!

*For more information on the God/Savior Complex, see the article *The Savior Complex: Why good intentions may have negative outcomes* in Psychology Today and the article *Always Trying to 'Save' People? You Might Have a Savior Complex* on the healthline.com website.[5]*

---

[5] https://www.healthline.com/health/savior-complex, accessed 08/26/21.

THE SILENCE OF GOD

One of the hardest things to deal with when we go through life's challenges is the silence of God. The silence of God is one of the most used reasons that people develop a God/Savior Complex; this occurs not because of any error on the part of God, but because of a deficiency of faith on our part. It is a natural response to panic when challenges come our way. It is also natural to become stressed and to feel alone, but we must realize that we are not alone and that God's silence is not a call for us to take matters into our own hands. Neither is it an indication that God has left us or has no concern for what troubles us. On the contrary, God very much cares about us and what concerns us, and the silence of God serves a divine and loving purpose.

While matriculating through graduate school and wrestling with my dissertation, I went through a frustrating period of life. It stressed me out and what added to the stress was the fact that God was being silent. It was during this time that God (through a leader at my church) revealed something to me. That revelation not only changed my perception of the situation I was going through, but it also forever changed my life and the way I comprehend the silence of God.

Here is that revelation: During our matriculation through any school system, we experience the stress of taking a test. From the moment we are first told about the test until it is finished and the grade is established, there is anxiety. Keep this in mind as I explain the revelation that came to me. Before any test, something very critical happens…**TEACHING**. Principal material is presented, practiced, reviewed, and executed repeatedly until it is expected that the student has learned that which has been taught. In our Christian walk, we are taught many things and tested on them all. I once had a pastor that said, "In life, you're either going into a storm, currently in a storm, or just coming out of one." Let's substitute the word TEST for the word STORM. In life you are either going into a test, currently in a test, or just coming out of a test, and no matter which position you are in, you may find yourself experiencing the silence of God.

Now, you may be asking yourself, why would God be silent when I need God the most? Here's why. Because **the teacher never speaks during a test!** God is so confident in you and in the lessons that He has taught that He has no reason to speak during the test. WOW! How amazing is that? What a liberating revelation! When God is silent, it is because He knows that we already have all the answers we need to pass the test. It is up to us to remove ourselves from the distractions of life and get into the stillness of God so that we can recall those answers. Think about it, we think better and more clearly when it is quiet.

Here is yet another parallel between earthly tests and heavenly tests: **we need quiet to think**. It is in the silence that we can feel the presence of God and recall the lessons of God. Always remember that: **just because the teacher is silent, that doesn't mean that the teacher isn't still with us.** What a wonderful comfort that the words of God through Moses to the Israelites are still true for us today: "...[God] will never leave you nor forsake you."[6] That means that

---

[6] Deuteronomy 31:6c and 31:8b, NIV version.

we can be sure that no matter what tests come our way, and no matter how alone we may feel, our Creator is **ALWAYS** with us and that will never change. The silence of God is not indicative of the absence of God. When we need help God is always there.

CHAPTER 3

Jesus Is Not Fire Retardant

Did you know that there are people who believe they are saved, but they are not. Yes, they have been baptized and may even be faithful members of a local congregation, but they are merely practicing idolatry. They have literally turned Jesus into an idol. Now, you may be asking, "How is that possible?" You might also be asking, "How can someone turn God into an idol?" The answer is simple: by using Jesus (God) as fire retardant or hell repellent instead of having a relationship with him as the LORD. It is the difference of **religion** versus **relationship**. To serve God out of mere habit is not enough to get a person into heaven. Doing everything right or being a good person doesn't mean that a person is saved from an eternity in hell. And yes, hell is real!

All too often, we mistake the meekness of Christ as weakness and the love of Christ as a reason to cheapen the grace that we have only through him. There are people and even preachers and pastors who truly believe that "A loving God/Savior wouldn't send people to hell." This is a dangerous theology because while God (and Jesus) are loving, merciful, and gracious, they are also **JUST**. And even on our best day, it is impossible for a person to be **good enough** all by themselves without the help of God/Christ.

Here's another truth: heaven is a **choice** and so is hell. God doesn't put us in either place without our first choosing, through free-will, to be there. This means that those who willingly choose eternal death through disobedience and faithlessness will obtain just that: eternal death in the lake of fire. Conversely, those who choose eternal life through faith in Jesus Christ and faithful obedience will ultimately receive their choice: an eternity in heaven. Another truth is we can't live any kind of way and expect to receive all of the blessings and glory promised only to those who have kept the faith and been obedient to God.

Remember, the Bible says, "Do not be deceived; God is not mocked, for you reap whatever you sow. If you sow to your own flesh, you will reap corruption from the flesh; but if you sow to the Spirit, you will reap eternal life from the Spirit."[7] This means that God gave you free will, and God is loving enough not to take it away from you. Whatever you choose, you will reap the consequences of that choice. So, if you choose eternal LIFE, you will reap the consequence of eternal life thereto appertaining, and if you choose eternal DEATH, you will reap the consequences of eternal death in the lake of fire.

So, you see, it's not God who *sends* people to hell. It's that people *choose* to go to hell through their disobedience and lack of faith. This is why the Bible says, "I call heaven and earth to witness against you today that I have set before you life and death, blessings

---

[7] Galatians 6:7-8, NRSV version.

and curses. Choose life so that you and your descendants may live, loving the Lord your God, obeying [God], and holding fast to [God]; for that means life to you and length of days...."[8] Everyday, we are asked to make a choice: choose life or choose death, choose blessings or curses. I recommend you choose **LIFE**!

---

[8] Deuteronomy 30:19-20b NRSV version.

A SURE SALVATION

Let's go back and talk about those who think they are saved, think they have chosen life, but in reality, they are hell and eternal death bound. These are those who have cheapened God's grace and have believed the bad theology that "Once saved, always saved." There are those who started out in faith, once chose life, and then for whatever reason, they turned away. As a result, they have disqualified themselves from receiving the heavenly prize they once labored for. The author of the book of Hebrews says it this way:

"For if we willfully persist in sin after having received the knowledge of the truth, there no longer remains a sacrifice for sins, but a fearful prospect of judgment, and a fury of fire that will consume the adversaries."[9]

Furthermore, Jesus says this about those who think they are saved but are not:

"Not everyone who says to me, 'Lord, Lord,' will enter the kingdom of heaven, but only the one who does the will of my Father in heaven. On that day many will say to me, 'Lord, Lord, did we not prophesy in your name, and cast out demons in your name, and do many deeds of power in your name?' Then I will declare to them, 'I never knew you; go away from me, you evildoers.'"[10]

---

[9] Hebrews 10:26-28, NRSV version.
[10] Matthew 7:21-23, NRSV version.

You see, true salvation is about heart service not just lip service; it's about relationship, not just religion. Just like with our human relationships, knowing **OF** someone is not the same as really **KNOWING** that person. Our relationship with Jesus as our LORD and SAVIOR is no different. It is not enough to just know OF Him through mindless religious acts (like those mentioned in Matthew 7:22). In order for him to know us, we have to truly get to know him through an intimate relationship with him and that type of relationship can only come from giving our whole heart to him. Just going to church and being a good person is not enough to ensure one's soul salvation.

Here is the bottom line: **Jesus will not be our savior if he is not first our Lord!** No one is afforded the benefits of salvation without having first made Jesus LORD over their life. That means, you have to completely sell out to him and him alone. And the most wonderful reality is this God (Jesus) doesn't just want to date you. No, God wants an eternal relationship with you! Jesus wants to literally MARRY you as part of his holy bride **the church.** So, if you are now wondering whether or not you are truly saved, take the time right now to pray for the blessed assurance of knowing that your soul will be with God after this life is over. Pray a prayer of salvation[11] and commit your whole heart to Christ from this day forward.

---

[11] A number of salvation prayers can be found on the internet through a search engine like google.com. Find the one that best fits what your heart wants to say and pray it earnestly. Then contact a Bible based church and let them know that you have a salvation prayer; they will give you the next steps to take.

CHAPTER 4

The Danger of "Turn and tell your neighbor...."

Have you ever been sitting in a church service and heard a preacher say something like, "Turn and tell your neighbor...," or "High five your neighbor and say..." For some reason, this has become such a common occurrence in worship services that it is even parodied in movies, sitcoms, and books. You may be asking, "What's so bad about saying what the preacher says to say?" I'm glad you asked. Here's the deal and the truth: words have power AND lying is never a God-approved behavior.

I'm sure that like other traditions and fads that have turned into bad habits or even dangerous theologies, this one started out as a harmless ploy to get and keep worshipers engaged in the service and the sermon that was going forth. Nevertheless, over time, "Tell your neighbor..." has become the toe-hole for a dangerous theology that teaches our parishioners to blindly believe everything that comes from the pulpit without question or analysis. "Tell you neighbor..." has also led to the dangerous theology of expecting or viewing every statement from the pulpit as a sign from God, especially if it evokes a physical or emotional response in the listener.

These theologies are dangerous for a number of reasons. First, they make the assumption that the person in the pulpit is infallible and that their words and deeds are beyond reproach or contestation because they are equal to God. This way of thinking completely bypasses the fact that the person in the pulpit is just that; a PERSON, a fallible, imperfect human being. Secondly, they ignore the fact that although the person in the pulpit is supposed to be a spokesperson of God and their words are supposed to be inspired and divinely timed by God, the sad fact is that this is not always the case. Thirdly, these theologies are dangerous because they can lead to ethically, spiritually, and emotionally negative consequences. These theologies are also dangerous because they can lead to brainwashed parishioners. And lastly, they can lead to parishioners putting church leaders on a metaphorical pedestal, thus making idols out of church leaders which can cause our parishioners to begin to think of every word from the pulpit that causes a physical response like shivers or chills as a sign that if it feels right or good and sounds right or good, then it must be from God, or it must be confirmation from God. The dangerous theologies that have come from "Tell your neighbor..." have given birth to cynical Christians and skeptical churchgoers; people who are looking for and needing the truth, but are instead receiving dressed up lies for the sake of entertainment.

Some of the above reasons may seem a little far fetched or absurd, but if we really think about it, we can think of examples where the above reasons have become a sad reality. This is because when we are at our lowest or most desperate, we tend to grab onto any crumb of hope, even if it is merely an illusion. We look for signs, confirmations, hints from God, or answers anywhere we think we may be able to find them. We become more susceptible to well sounding words and craftily worded lies. Lies that over the years (albeit said with good intentions) have caused people to doubt God and even to become so angry at God that they no longer want anything more to do with Him. Lies that sound so good that they have become part of the norm in religious rhetoric. Examples of such lies are as follows:

If God did it for me, He will do it for you.

If you want it, you can have it.

Name it, and claim it, and it will be yours.

If you believe hard enough, it will happen.

If you pray hard enough (or often enough) it will come to pass.

If you feel strongly about it, that's confirmation from God.

If you say it (or see it) before it becomes reality, it will become reality.

Your blessing is on the way.

This is your season (or this is your time).

It's your turn for a blessing.

God says….

You're next in line for a blessing.

God is always on your side.

Here's the truth: God is too big to be put into a box and too powerful to be cajoled or manipulated into doing our will when and how we want it done. God is sovereign and behaves in ways that are best, and that will bring Him the most glory. What's more, as leaders, we have to be careful to not speak on behalf of God presumptuously. If God has not spoken, then we too must be silent. God's thoughts and ways are so beyond our understanding that it is foolish to try to predict how and when God will act at any point in time. Therefore, even when spoken in faith or with great conviction and well intentions, the words we as church leaders say need to be filtered through the Holy Spirit and not tradition, nor through our own desires. To be the church that Jesus envisioned and the kind of church that the wounded of the world need, we must yield our words to truth and not mere tradition, accepting, and teaching our parishioners to accept, the glorious (and sometimes beautiful) mystery of God's sovereignty.

CHAPTER 5

Necessary Pain

There are some moments in life that are harder than words can describe. Times that are so hard they are literally painful. The crazy thing about these times is that they are not always caused by the enemy, but rather, they are caused or allowed by God. Just look at the story of Job. The hardship that Job faced was caused by the devil but commissioned and allowed by God in order to bring about a greater version of Job and a greater understanding of who God truly is for both Job and his friends. This biblical fact teaches us that the enemy has to obtain permission from our sovereign and all-powerful God before attacking us.

To that end, this chapter is for all of those who are experiencing the hard, rough, complicated, frustrating, or disappointing times in life that challenge your faith. This chapter is also for those who are angry with, pissed off at, mad at, disappointed in, or frustrated with God, for those who have felt let down or even failed by God. It is my sincere prayer that this chapter not only gives you peace and a greater understanding of the immense love that our God has for you, but that it will also restore and deepen your relationship with God.

To begin, let's look at some truths about God that are sometimes misunderstood. We have already discussed the fact that God's ways are not always our ways, nor are God's thoughts always like our thoughts. Both God's thoughts and actions are so far above our mere comprehension that there is no way any human could ever fully attain them. Think of it this way: picture a single ant crawling in the middle of China's Great Wall. The ant is only aware of its current point on the wall and perhaps where it has recently been, but the ant isn't aware of the total expanse of lives and space that exists beyond its current existence. Nevertheless, there is a great God, a master creator looking down on that ant who knows ALL that there is to know. This Creator knows everything about the ant's life, trials, challenges, expectations, hopes, natural enemies, and so much more! The ant continues to crawl on its way with only its goals in mind (likely the search for food). Meanwhile, there you are, in your everyday existence. Living your life, not a bit more conscious of that ant than it is of you, and yet the same God is watching over you both and providing for your needs.

Now, imagine yourself as that ant. Take into account all that you know about the world around you and the worlds beyond you. Now, realize that even with all of your vast knowledge, there is still so much more that you don't know. Can you describe in detail the life of someone on the other side of the planet? Can you describe in detail the expanse of heaven beyond the revelation of John in the Bible? What about the innermost desires of your neighbor's cousin? Do you know what that is? That last question may seem a little absurd, but guess what? God knows the answer to all of these questions and even knows how many hairs are on your head. In fact, not one of those hairs can fall out without God knowing it!

The truth is, God is BEYOND amazing and yet is so very personal that God is intimately involved in every aspect of your life, orchestrating your life like a great opus. From the beginning to the end, before you even took your first breath, God has been personally attentive to you. God is able to be just as personally attentive to every living creature, being, and article of creation all at the same time, without slighting one. Now **THAT** is **BEYOND** amazing! God doesn't just stand by or wind up your life and watch it play out however it will. No, God is active and involved in all of His creation.

So now, while keeping all of the above about God's attentiveness in mind, let's look at the hard moments of life. Those moments we would gladly erase if we had the option. In order to avoid giving birth to dangerous theologies or falling victim to them, there are some truths we need to remember. First of all, we all have free will. This free will is a gift from God, one that God will NEVER take away. You see, God's whole deal is that we choose God and God's kingdom willingly. He will never force Himself upon us, nor will God force us to do His will. However, God will make things uncomfortable enough to make choosing God and God's will more appealing, and yet there are still those who refuse. Thus, there will always be those who choose evil and death over obedience and life. Nevertheless, those who choose evil, like Judas who betrayed Jesus and like the tares that grew up with the wheat in the parable of the wheat and tares, even they have and serve a divine purpose. I know that may sound strange for a holy God to use unholy people and deeds for divine purposes, but we have to remember that God knows the full scope from eternity to eternity and has the best view of the bigger picture than we'll ever have. Now, that doesn't mean that God will always prevent bad things from happening to us, nor will God always stand in the way of those who wish to do us harm, but one thing we can depend on is that God has promised to take what a human means for evil and still turn it around for our good.

All of the above being said, when we experience hard and even traumatic times, we must remember that God is still present, still protecting, and still working on our side to make even the worst of situations work out for our good. I'm not just telling you what sounds good, but rather I am speaking from experience–hard fought experiences that God has indeed turned around for my good. Remember, God always keeps His promises and has never and will never ever fail. There is purpose in what you have gone through and it will work out for your good, according to Romans 8:28.

BROKEN WITH GRACE

Let me now pose a question to you, dear reader: Does God cause pain? Many have debated this question and the answer might surprise you. The answer is yes! Anyone who tells you differently is lying and spreading a dangerous theology. Also, not all pain caused by God is the result of sin or punishment. Remember, God is just, merciful, gracious, loving, kind, and **not at all** petty. The truth is that some pain is caused as a result of punishment, but some pain is caused as a byproduct of spiritual growth. Yes, spiritual growth pains are just as real as physical growth pains, and sometimes just as painful if not more. The unfortunate truth is that there is no ibuprofen or pain killer to numb the pain of spiritual growth. The pain of spiritual growth is something we all have to go through and that we all have experienced at one time or another.

In painful moments, whether they be brought on as a result of punishment or for the purpose of spiritual growth, or if the pain is the result of both reasons together, it is important to remember that God never causes pain without grace and love. Again, God is never petty or tyrannical, rather God is merciful, gracious, loving, and just. This being said, during painful times, remember that...

"...discipline always seems painful rather than pleasant at the time, but later it yields the peaceful fruit of righteousness to those who have been trained by it."[12]

---

[12] Hebrews 12:11

This means that when painful moments arise in our lives, when we find ourselves broken from the inside out, there is still a reason to rejoice and give God praise because there is indeed purpose in the pain and promotion in the process no matter how grievous. God deals with us as a good parent to a child, and what is best for us will not always feel the best, but even when we aren't sure about God's methods, we can be sure that God's motives are always steeped in love and grace.

(As a side note: When I am experiencing pain through spiritual growth or even punishment, the two gospel songs that minister to me most in those hard times are *Gracefully Broken* by Tasha Cobbs Leonard and *Father Knows Best* by Kirk Franklin.[13] I invite you to listen to and meditate on the lyrics of these songs as you go through the painful moments of your life, and remember that God's love is behind it all, and that no pain lasts forever, this season, like all others, will pass.)

---

[13] I do not own the rights to these songs. I merely mention them as examples.

CHAPTER 6

I Got Questions!

Have you ever been in a spiritual crisis or a crisis of life and felt that you had more questions than answers, only to have someone tell you not to question God? As an inquisitive child and now as an inquisitive adult, one of the most annoying things to me was to have people in church (including my own mother) tell me, "Don't question God." This statement used to frustrate me because I couldn't understand why a God who was almighty and loving couldn't handle someone like me asking him a question, especially since there are a number of people in the Bible that asked God questions. For goodness sakes, Job spent like 30 chapters asking God questions! Even Jesus asked God while being crucified, "My God, my God, why have you forsaken me?" I came to the conclusion that people who say "Don't question God" have put God in a metaphorical box and painted Him as either being too feeble to answer questions or too tyrannical to entertain questions from His lowly and unworthy subjects. Neither of these views of God are accurate, and frankly, neither are the picture of a God I would want to serve.

Given all the biblical evidence of people asking God questions, and given the fact that when we pray, we ask God for the things we want and need, the phrase "Don't question God!" never made a lot of sense to me. And as I said, it frustrated me as a believer. Now, you or someone you know may feel or have felt the same way I did. You or someone you know may still feel that way. Today, I want you to know a liberating truth: **God can handle your questions!** It's true. The God we serve is big enough and loving enough to answer any question you throw His way. What's more, God actually welcomes questions and desires for you to ask them. In addition, God doesn't just want us to ask questions that request something, God wants us to ask questions for greater understanding. James 1:5 says: "If any of you is lacking in wisdom, ask God, who gives to all generously and ungrudgingly, and it will be given to you."

You may be asking yourself, "What about other questions?" I fully believe that God is able to deal with all types of questions. When examining the biblical book of Job, we see Job asking questions like: "Why?", "Where are you?", "What do I need to learn?", "Why are you doing this to me?", "What have I done to deserve this?", "Why was I even born?", "Why have you let me live, only to kill me?", "Why have you made an enemy out of me?", and so on. In fact, Job was so open and honest with his questions that he bared his soul for all who would to hear (and read). He was in such a desperate place that he couldn't allow mere habitual religiosity to hinder his getting to God and getting the answers and peace that he needed (although they didn't come in the form he was looking for).

So, where did Job go wrong with his questions? Or did he? Well, the answer to the question of Job's error or errors is a debated one.

Nevertheless, after all of Job's questioning, after all of Job's complaints, and after all of Job's moments of self-pity, the only expressed error that the LORD utters against Job is that he has spoken in ignorance about things that are beyond his comprehension, thus showing a lack of faith and trust in the sovereignty, wisdom, and love of God. In Job 38:2, God finally answers Job, and the first thing God says isn't "How dare you question me!" No, God handles Job with the grace and compassion of a God who knew exactly who Job was and understood exactly what Job had been through. And the comforting thing for us to remember is that when we have questions, our loving God will deal with us in the same way: with love, grace, compassion, and understanding.

Here's the bottom line and the most important thing to remember: God our creator and lover of our soul is open to our questions and is willing to provide the answers we need as God sees fit, and if not, God will always provide the peace we need to make it through even our toughest of times without those answers. Nonetheless, it behooves us to remember our place when asking God questions. I believe the point of the statement "Don't question God!" is more of an admonishment not to question God's sovereignty or authority to do whatever God wills to do. It is also an admonishment not to question God's motive or heart condition for doing what God does. The statement "Don't question God!" is, in my opinion, a challenge to have faith in the immense and eternal love that God has for us. Afterall, once we believe and understand that we can always trust God's heart, trusting God's sovereignty becomes easier.

CHAPTER 7

The End?

As I stated before, this book was never intended to contain an exhaustive list of all of the bad or dangerous theologies that are circulating among Christian believers today. Neither was this book meant to be a criticism of the church, but rather this book is meant to shed light on some of the dangerous traditional teachings that lead to dangerous theologies. Furthermore, my goal in writing this book is to ignite a spark and desire in the hearts of church leaders for a better quality of theological and spiritual education for our congregations.

That being said, I am confident that this is not the end of this discussion. There is so much more to discuss and debate when it comes to traditional teachings that can lead to dangerous theologies, and unfortunately, new bad teachings and dangerous theologies are being formed and perpetuated all the time. And while none of us has all of the answers to what is right and what is wrong, all of us have the challenge to study and pursue that which is true, just, right, loving, and so forth.

As believers and church leaders it should be our quest and goal to teach the people of God and those with itching ears the truth and not merely something that sounds good or that which is trending at the time. Afterall, as it says in James 3:1 we who teach will be judged more severely. Why? Because the lives, theologies, and wellbeing of those who listen to us hang on our vary words, and their relationship with God can be abundantly helped or harmed by what we say and do.

Conclusion

Hopefully, you have learned the importance of researching biblical facts for yourself instead of merely depending on the word of another person. Hopefully, you have also learned that tradition without wisdom and knowledge can be very dangerous, and that just because something sounds right or catchy, it doesn't mean that it's a fact, nor does it mean that it should be repeated. Finally, I hope that we have all learned that we as leaders must pay close attention to the teaching we perpetuate and that we allow ourselves to utter in the presence of God's people. Words matter! And as church leaders we are responsible for their effects on our congregations and communities. We have to remember that words travel far and fast, and they won't merely linger in our sanctuaries after people have gone home. All of the above being said, when we speak, let us think not only of what we are saying, but also of those to whom our words may travel.

Also, I hope that you have learned that the things we hear, see, and experience in our everyday lives help to form our lives and understandings of God and God's relationship to this world and all therein. These bits of understanding are what ultimately come together to form what is called our embedded theology. This embedded theology, whether we are Christians or not, becomes the engrained framework through which we interpret life and the world around us. Unfortunately, too many bad experiences and too many run-ins with shifty people and, or bad teachings can cause us to inadvertently develop bad and even dangerous theologies; theologies that cause more harm than good.

Dangerous theologies can easily lead to church—hurt, life-hurt, theological disappointments, crises of faith and more. Everyone knows that in life we go through moments of hurt, disappointment, trauma, etcetera, but dangerous theologies can make these moments much worse; especially when it seems as though we have no one to turn to for help, not even God. In those times, our relationship with God can become strained and even (at worst) non-existent, leading us to try to find another way to cope in order to survive. Ways, like self-medicating with drugs, alcohol, food, sex, a combination of these, or something worse. Another way one might try to cope is by withdrawing from church, friends, family, and, or society in general. That withdrawal can eventually lead to feelings of depression, loneliness, anxiety, and even feelings or thoughts of suicide or self-harm.

Truly it is nice to think the everyday with God (Jesus) gets sweeter as the days go by, but the truth is that some days are not sweet. Some days are confusing, infuriating, bitter, hurtful, or just plain bad. Yes, bad days in our relationship with God can and do happen. Nevertheless, there is so much good and so much love surrounding even the worst of days, in the grand scheme of things, the good days really do outweigh the bad days. However, if you are a person whose relationship with God has been strained because of dangerous theologies; it is my hope that you will give God another chance, and know that God's love for you is big enough to take your anger, sadness, disappointment, pain, and more and love you through and in spite of it all.

The hope that remains, after becoming the victim of dangerous theologies, is that God is always there to heal us and love us through the mess of it all. Not only that, but God will also clean the mess up, clean us up, and somehow through it all, make all that we have suffered through work out for our good. There really is light at the end of the tunnel, and it is not that of an oncoming train. It is the light of hope and love.

Here's the bottom line: if we as Christian leaders adhere to the advice that Paul gave to his protégé Timothy in 1 Timothy 4:16a: "Pay close attention to yourself and to your teaching...." we will not only be able to break the course of perpetuated ignorance, we will also be able to save our listeners from developing and engaging in dangerous theologies.

About the Author

Dr. Alicia C. Tulloss is a native of Nashville, Tennessee. She matriculated from preschool to high school here in the city of Nashville and went on to pursue her Bachelor Degree in Agriculture at the University of Tennessee at Knoxville. From there she went on to further her education at the Interdenominational Theological Center in Atlanta Georgia, gaining both a Master of Divinity in Pastoral Care and Counseling (Psychology of Religion) and a Doctor of Ministry degree with a specialty in Pastoral Counseling. In 2006, she was inducted into the International Honor Society of Theta Phi. In 2013 she completed her dissertation entitled: *The Pastoral Care Professional As Pastoraldramist and Holistic Caregiver: Addressing The Churchgoing Experiences of Black Youth Through Pastoral Care and Psychodrama.*

DR. A. C. TULLOSS

In 2008, Dr. Tulloss began assistant teaching with Christian Worship classes at the Interdenominational Theological Center and found a new passion in Theological Education. She has since continued to teach, preach, write, and speak for the purpose of educating, equipping, and empowering God's people. Also, in 2008 under the pastorship of Dr. Aaron L. Parker, Dr. Tulloss was licensed to minister the Christian gospel around the world. Exodus 3:5 in connection with Isaiah 52:7 have served to undergird her convictions concerning ministry. Following her calling as a true and anointed servant she is known for always preaching barefoot.

NOTES

NOTES

NOTES

NOTES

NOTES

NOTES

NOTES

NOTES

NOTES

NOTES

NOTES

www.ingramcontent.com/pod-product-compliance
Lightning Source LLC
Chambersburg PA
CBHW070938120626
46546CB00004B/1466